Keep Your Pantheon

by David Mamet

A SAMUEL FRENCH ACTING EDITION

FOUNDED 1830

New York Hollywood London Toronto

SAMUELFRENCH.COM

IMPORTANT BILLING AND CREDIT REQUIREMENTS

Center Theatre Group
L.A.'s Theatre Company

Ahmanson Theatre
Mark Taper Forum
Kirk Douglas Theatre

Michael Ritchie, ARTISTIC DIRECTOR **Charles Dillingham**, MANAGING DIRECTOR
Gordon Davidson, FOUNDING ARTISTIC DIRECTOR

Presents

TWO UNRELATED PLAYS
BY
DAVID MAMET

KEEP YOUR PANTHEON [2008]

AND

THE DUCK VARIATIONS [1971]

With (IN ALPHABETICAL ORDER)

Jeffrey Addiss   Michael Cassidy   Steven Goldstein   Harold Gould
Vincent Guastaferro   Dominic Hoffman   J.J. Johnston   Michael Lerner   Rod McLachlan
Ed O'Neill   David Paymer   Jonathan Rossetti   Jack Wallace

Set Design	Costume Design	Lighting Design	Sound Design
Takeshi Kata	**Ilona Somogyi**	**Christopher Akerlind**	**Cricket S. Myers**

Casting	Associate Producer	Production Stage Manager	Stage Manager
Bonnie Grisan	**Kelley Kirkpatrick**	**David S. Franklin**	**Elizabeth Atkinson**

Directed by
Neil Pepe

May 11 – June 8, 2008
Kirk Douglas Theatre

Keep Your Pantheon is a World Premiere Production

The Duck Variations and *Keep Your Pantheon* are generously supported in part
by Artistic Director's Circle member John S. Surabian Jr., and in memory of
Faith and Sharon Ann Surabian.

KEEP YOUR PANTHEON

BY
DAVID MAMET

DIRECTED BY NEIL PEPE

THE CAST
(IN ALPHABETICAL ORDER)

Jeffrey Addiss	Ensemble
Michael Cassidy	Philius
Steven Goldstein	Quintus Magnus
Vincent Guastaferro	Herald
Dominic Hoffman	Lupus Albus Secundus
J.J. Johnston	Titus
Rod McLachlan	Messenger, Ensemble
Ed O'Neill	Strabo
David Paymer	Pelargon
Jonathan Rossetti	Ensemble
Jack Wallace	Ramus

THE SCENE
An actors studio in ancient Rome.

*This play is
dedicated
to Jack Wallace*

Scene One

(AT RISE: AN ACTORS STUDIO IN ANCIENT ROME.)

(Two actors, STRABO and PELARGON, in ratty togas are batting their arms, trying to keep warm. Walking up and down.)

(Outside, in the rain, a HERALD walks by the open windows.)

HERALD. O for the tongues of all the gods To decry that fate, which 'gainst all odds Has Brought the Tenth African Legion Low Oh, Rome, rend your garments and ashes throw...

STRABO. Has anybody seen my codpiece...?

HERALD. Has brought the Tenth African Legion low...

PELARGON. *(to the HERALD)* Hey, what happened to the Tenth African Legion?

HERALD. The Tenth African Legion has suffered its first defeat...

STRABO. "Mee, me, mo mo moo moo..." Has anybody seen my lucky codpiece...?

HERALD. They have suffered their first defeat Loss is more bitter than victory's sweet.

STRABO. "Mmee mee hah mah..." Would you, *would* you, give a working man a break.

HERALD. Buy Sosostris Sandals – the Egyptians wore them. They *just don't wear out!*

STRABO. Has anybody –

PELARGON. You don't need your codpiece to do your voice exercises.

STRABO. I don't work without my codpiece.

PELARGON. The kid is not going to be impressed by your codpiece.

STRABO. Where is he?

PELARGON. He went out to get the mail.

STRABO. IN THE RAIN? YOU LET HIM GO OUT IN THE RAIN?

(The kid, **PHILIUS,** *enters sopping wet and sneezes.)*

PHILIUS. Achoo.

STRABO. Young Philius, may I assist you out of those Wet Clothes…?

PELARGON. *(to self)* …oh, please.

STRABO. *(***PHILIUS** *sneezes.)* And are you unwell?

PHILIUS. *(quoting)* "What is the health of this mineral body, compared to the health of Rome?"

STRABO. That's *very* good.

PELARGON. It's "mortal body," not "mineral body."

STRABO. He *said* "mortal body."

PELARGON. I can't understand a thing he's saying.

STRABO. He's getting a *cold*, alright? And pee ess. Any *dolt* can "say the words." *He's* got the *feeling.*

*(***PHILIUS** *sneezes.)*

Give him a cup of wine.

PELARGON. It's our last wine.

STRABO. And are we not to share it with our *student?* With that youth who has so esteemed us, as to leave his home, and apply to us for instruction…? Who has thrown his lot in with us. In pursuit of that Most Noble of Achievements; Service of *Thalia,* the Muse of Comedy. God *bless* you, Youngster. How it delights These Old Bones to feel the *warmth* of your enthusiasms. May our years together…

*(***PHILIUS** *shows a letter.)*

PHILIUS. Strabo, I have a letter for you.

STRABO. Who is the letter from?

PHILIUS. My father.

STRABO. Ah. And has he sent your tuition?

PHILIUS. No. He says I have to come home.

(pause)

STRABO. Why?

PHILIUS. Because, you said you'd put me on the stage – and since I've arrived, you haven't had a job.

(pause)

And you said you'd put me on stage.

STRABO. And I *shall* put you on stage. WHERE YOU BELONG. *But.* One must have patience.

PHILIUS. And we don't have enough to eat.

STRABO. It's the Spartan Method. We've explained the Spartan Method.

PHILIUS. *(as water falls on his head.)* And the roof is leaking.

STRABO. Philius, the service of our Muse is hard. But Fortune favors fortitude. How we will laugh, in times to come at what will, in that happy hour, be seen as less-than-inconveniences.

PHILIUS. Oh, and I have another letter.

STRABO. *(as PELARGON hands him the letter)* What is it?

PELARGON. *(reads)* It's an inquiry of our Availability.

STRABO. An inquiry of our Availability. You see! You see! We *are* available. The Day is *saved.* Fortune has smiled on our Steadfastness. *Write* your father. Tell him we are employed.

PHILIUS. I'm happy, Strabo.

STRABO. I know that you are. *(to PELARGON)* See how the merest brief emotions pursue each other o'er the bright plasticity of his manly face.

(It rains on them.)

PHILIUS. Should I go up and fix the leak?

PELARGON. How would you fix it?

PHILIUS. I could find out where it's coming from.

PELARGON. I believe it's coming from the roof.

PHILIUS. I believe so, too. "And I praise Mighty Zeus, for that bright happy wind which…"

PELARGON. "Steered me…"

STRABO. *He* knows it…*he* knows it…

PHILIUS. "Steered me to this refuge. O Athena, send your seed of wisdom to search through the rock of my innards."

PELARGON. Amen, with all my heart.

(*PHILIUS exits.*)

STRABO. The lad *has* something – don't you think?

PELARGON. He'll never go to bed with you.

STRABO. His reluctance, to date, I lay at the feet of poverty.

(*taking the letter*)

With the belly full "love will bloom like the wild gorse on Mount Ida." The Sicilian Cork Festival!!!

PELARGON. (*taking the letter*) The *Lesser* Sicilian Cork Festival.

STRABO. Are not the Lesser Sicilians entitled to amusement...? When does our engagement begin?

PELARGON. It's not an engagement. It's an *audition.*

STRABO. An audition...?

PELARGON. Yes.

STRABO. They want me to come to Sicily to AUDITION?

PELARGON. (*reads; showing the letter*) "The proctors of The Lesser Sicilian Cork Festival are pleased to announce that you have been selected as one of the THIRTY troops invited to audition..."

STRABO. I? *Strabo?*

PELARGON. *Yes.*

STRABO. *Strabo?* Who played before Caesar...?

PELARGON. ...as a child...

STRABO. Who reduced the Neapolitan Senate to tears...

PELARGON. (*simultaneous*) "...reduced the Neapolitan Senate to tears..."

STRABO. To whom, this Gifted lad, this *comet,* has applied for instruction? He *could* have gone to the Company of Paulus, may his name be accursed. No. But he did not *go* to the Company of Paulus. No – he came *here...*to work beneath me...

PELARGON. Dream on.

STRABO. And, these *swine* ask me: to "audition," to "plead," to be allowed to play the...*what* is it?

PELARGON. ...the Lesser Sicilian.

STRABO. The Lesser Sicilian *Cork* Festival? While Paulus, *that hack*, in my rightful place, performs before Caesar.

PELARGON. Well, not now he doesn't, cause he's in Sardinia.

STRABO. May he remain there. Entertaining Savages.

(*Door opens, enter* **RAMUS**, *an old drunk*)

RAMUS. By the gods.

PELARGON. By the gods.

STRABO. Not today.

RAMUS. I seek no charity...I come with...

STRABO. Yes, I know. Charms, and portents, potions and news. Not tod...

RAMUS. A love charm...

STRABO. I don't require a love charm.

RAMUS. I saw the kid on the roof.

STRABO. I don't require a love charm to succeed with the kid.

RAMUS. How long's he been with you?

STRABO. He's *shy*, alright, the lad's shy...

RAMUS. A fetish, a *token*, which I will *trade*, for one cup of wine.

STRABO. Absolutely not.

RAMUS. I have a *token* to dispel bad luck.

STRABO. No.

RAMUS. One cup of wine...

STRABO. Go away.

RAMUS. *This charm* was given to me, by the Great Lupus Albus, White Wolf of Sardinia, when we served in the Tenth African Legion.

STRABO. You served in the Tenth African Legion?

RAMUS. I served beside him. In the Snows.

PELARGON. What was the Tenth African Legion doing in the Snows?

RAMUS. We were lost.

> *(pause)*

And I need a drink.

STRABO. That's quite a shock.

RAMUS. Because I'm having a particularly hard day.

PELARGON. Why is that?

RAMUS. *Because* I have just heard they have suffered defeat.

STRABO. Who has suffered defeat?

RAMUS. The Tenth African Legion. My comrades...have suffered their first defeat...

STRABO. You were never in the Tenth African Legion.

PHILIUS. *(reentering; drenched)* Strabo...

STRABO. *(to PHILIUS)* You look lovely when you're wet.

PHILIUS. Thank you, Strabo.

STRABO. What did you want to tell me?

PHILIUS. The landlord's coming.

PELARGON. Oh, no.

PHILIUS. *(exiting)* I'm going to change my clothes.

STRABO. *(to PHILIUS)* Put on something revealing.

> *(Enter the landlord, QUINTUS MAGNUS)*

QUINTUS. By the gods.

PELARGON. By the gods.

STRABO. *(to RAMUS)* We are honored, Sir. We are honored. That you chose us.

QUINTUS. Strabo.

STRABO. Quintus. You shouldn't be out in this weather. One moment –

> *(to RAMUS)*

...Chose *us*, Sir, over...

> *(to QUINTUS)*

He could have hired the Troop of Paulus.

QUINTUS. Strabo...

STRABO. He could have hired the Troop of Paulus, beloved of Caesar...

QUINTUS. Strabo.

STRABO. But this man of taste chose *us*.

QUINTUS. Your rent is four months overdue...

STRABO. We would have brought it to you, but for this accursed rain...

QUINTUS. *I* came out in the rain...

STRABO. You're a bold man, and I applaud you for it.

PHILIUS. *(returning; a towel over his head)* Achoo.

QUINTUS. The child looks *dreadful*...

STRABO. I would have come, even *given* the rain – but for my understandable anxiety. My new lead, here, young Philius, has caught a cold. Which, Zeus forfend, might *might* prohibit him from performing in the upcoming festival for which we've been engaged.

QUINTUS. You've got a job?

STRABO. This, this man of discernment has come to engage us to open the Sicilian Cork Festival.

(pause)

QUINTUS. The Sicilian Cork Festival...

STRABO. The honorarium for which will, thank you for waiting, discharge our debts, and restore my troupe, in the eyes of the world, to that position it deserves.

QUINTUS. You're going to sail to Sicily?

STRABO. In his private Trireme.

QUINTUS. This fellow looks like a beggar.

STRABO. Which disguise, Sir, has kept him safe, rich as he is, rich as Marcus Rufus *Cronax*, through travels, through his vast possessions, throughout the Known World. *Thank* you for your forebearance, Quintus.

PHILIUS. We're going to Sicily, Strabo...?

QUINTUS. Before you go, would you pay the rent?

STRABO. Upon the instant. Let me but collect an advance upon the swingeing fee this fine man has offered.

*(They turn to **RAMUS**, who is now asleep. Pause.)*

STRABO. Hush, thinking again. Do not wake him. For he has come, battered by the storm, from far-off Sicily. And the journey has fatigued him. Let our benefactor sleep. Sleep on, oh Patron of the Arts.

QUINTUS. Fifty sesterces. Tomorrow morning.

STRABO. When I shall come, Sir, with this good man's "stipend," in my pocket placing it, *gently*, no, but not without a sense of triumph, in your sweating hands.

QUINTUS. Or, I'm going to sic the bailiffs on you.

STRABO. How we'll laugh, tomorrow morning. Recalling those intemperate words…

QUINTUS. By the gods.

PELARGON. By the gods.

(**QUINTUS** *exits into the storm.*)

PHILIUS. We're going to Sicily, Strabo…?

STRABO. (*to* **PELARGON**) Wake him up.

PHILIUS. Because, if we are, I'm going to need some new clothes.

PELARGON. What is our plan…?

STRABO. It's not a "plan," Pelargon. It is known as a "plot." Which, as we are taught, is based upon human *motivation.*

PELARGON. And what is the motivation?

STRABO. *Greed.* Tomorrow *morning…*

PELARGON. Tomorrow morning, the landlord doesn't get the rent, we go to debtor's prison.

STRABO. I shall give him something rather *better* than the rent.

PELARGON. What?

STRABO. "An unexpected *windfall.*" What man does not *prize* "an unexpected windfall?"

PELARGON. What is the windfall?

STRABO. We offer to *buy his building.* Ramus, this insanely wealthy gentleman from Sicily, offers to buy this pest-trap for some fabulous sum…

(*to* **RAMUS**)

Wake up.

PELARGON. And how do we *pay* for it?

STRABO. For what?

PELARGON. The building.

STRABO. Negotiations for the building, listen and learn, "drag on for months," this is called "buying time," during which time...

(to **RAMUS***)*

Wake up.

RAMUS. Trinkets, potions and news. I do not seek charity...

STRABO. Ramus, we have a job for you.

RAMUS. Make a small purchase. From an old soldier...

STRABO. Raa...

PELARGON. Buy something...

PHILIUS. Buy a charm, buy a charm, Strabo.

STRABO. Yes, yes, yes, *Ramus.* Oh, please. This charm, sell me this charm.

RAMUS. A fine choice, Sir, for *that* charm was a gift from Lupus Albus, the White Wolf of Sardinia, when we served in...

STRABO & RAMUS. *(simultaneous)* ...the Tenth African Legion

RAMUS. Which charm is warranted to immediately reverse ill-fortune.

STRABO. Accept this small coin with my thanks. Ramus: tomorrow morning, we're going to put on a little "play"...*You* will impersonate a Sicilian Lord...

PELARGON. How're we going to pass him off as a Sicilian Lord?

STRABO. *(stating the obvious)* We're going to show up with him drunk. As drunk as one after a night touring "Rome's Curious By-ways..." So drunk will he be that, in his drunkenness, he wants to buy this *pest-hole* for five times its worth.

PELARGON. Why?

STRABO. *(pause)* It reminds him of his aunt's house in Sardinia.

PHILIUS. You're very smart, Strabo.

STRABO. Study the Classics. Now, Ramus…

> *(A knocking is heard at the door. All turn.* **PHILIUS** *goes to the door.)*

VOICE. *(O.S.)* Open up!

STRABO. Oh, no.

PHILIUS. Who could be coming out in such a storm?

PELARGON. The bailiffs.

STRABO. The swine actually *sent* the bailiffs

VOICE. *(O.S.)* Open up!

STRABO. Alright. Tell them…*tell* them, we've gone.

PHILIUS. Where have we gone?

STRABO. To the Sicilian Cork Festival.

PELARGON. "Just when everything was going so well…"

> *(***PHILIUS*** *opens the door. A* **MESSENGER** *stands in the doorway.)*

MESSENGER. By the gods.

PELARGON. Oh, alright.

PHILIUS. Be welcome. To the Studio of Strabo. Sicily called them and they have responded, and, thus, are not here.

> *(pause)*

Belike they are elsewhere.

> *(pause)*

MESSENGER. *(pause) What* did you say?

STRABO. He said "The Studio of Strabo."

MESSENGER. Why does he talk like that?

STRABO. He has a cold.

MESSENGER. He said The Studio of Strabo?

STRABO. Yes.

MESSENGER. I *seek* the Studio of Strabo.

STRABO. You found it, but they aren't here.

MESSENGER. I had difficulty locating your house in the storm.

STRABO. A bailiff may not evict lawful tenants from their home between dusk and dawn.

MESSENGER. I'm...

STRABO. Tell him.

PELARGON. Section Three of the Pandects of Justinian.

(*PELARGON shrugs, meaning "I'm making it up, but who's gonna check."*)

MESSENGER. I've studied the Pandects of Justinian.

STRABO. As who has not.

MESSENGER. And I don't seem to...

STRABO. Get on with it.

MESSENGER. I represent Marcus Rufus Cronax. Richest man in Rome.

(*pause*)

STRABO. Marcus Cronax. Richest man in Rome?

MESSENGER. As I have said. Who had engaged an acting troupe. To perform this evening at his wife's festivities. They are unable to perform, and he sends to ask you to appear in their stead.

(*pause*)

The fee is meager, but six hundred sesterces, however...

STRABO. You wish us to perform *tonight*...

MESSENGER. We had engaged the Company of Gaius Paulus...

STRABO. You had engaged the Company of Gaius Paulus...

MESSENGER. But they have been lost at sea.

(*pause*)

STRABO. Oh gods, oh gods of fate, how we, from one dark moment to the next, stumble, grope and curse that which, with trust in *you* is revealed as a clear, shining path.

PELARGON. We'll be there.

MESSENGER. The loss of brother actors must come as a cruel shock...

STRABO. Paulus? Drowned? Where may we seek for consolation...?

MESSENGER. Paulus. Yes. And all his Company.

PELARGON. *Incredible* loss to the Theatrical World.

MESSENGER. ...the favorite actors of Caesar...

STRABO. After the engagement we will rend our flesh.

MESSENGER. Here are a list of the topics, they were to have dealt with at tonight's festivities...We have but the one question...

STRABO. State it.

MESSENGER. ...do you have *time* enough, to fashion a play, between now and sunset...?

STRABO. Sir, I am Strabo, who once improvised a two-hour ode...

MESSENGER. Oh. Where?

(*pause*)

PELARGON. At the Sicilian Cork Festival.

STRABO. (*to* **PELARGON**) Thank you.

MESSENGER. Here is the list of suggested topics. Do you know the house?

STRABO. Do I know the *house?*

MESSENGER. It is right next to the *armory.*

STRABO. Who does not know the house of Marcus Rufus Cronax!

MESSENGER. We expect you at sunset.

STRABO. "Can the sand stop the tide...?

MESSENGER. By the gods.

STRABO. Let us praise them with all our being.

(*The* **MESSENGER** *exits.*)

STRABO. (*does a Stop the Music*) Oh, ye gods, full of compassion who mete out to man not by his deserts, but by your immutable weights of Justice. Oh, ye gods, who *do* exist...

PHILIUS. But...

STRABO. Grant that the Troupe of Gaius Paulus, now taken to you, expired in prolonged agony.

PHILIUS. ...but.

STRABO. In the raging sea. What?

PHILIUS. But are we going to Sicily, Strabo?

STRABO. No, sweetheart, we're going to stay here and get rich.

Scene Two

(SCENE: *A STREET IN ANCIENT ROME – NIGHT – RAIN*)

(*The* HERALD *walks by.*)

HERALD. The Tenth African Legion in Ignominy
Shamed. Then the Troupe of Paulus drowned at sea.
The gods bid Rome within its doors to keep
Whilst the skies visage clouds, and een the heavens
weep, oh woe, oh woe

(*The* HERALD *passes by and the three actors take shelter beneath the overhang.* STRABO *is doing his vocal exercises.*)

STRABO. Oh, take it elsewhere.

HERALD. Peloponnesian Syrup of Myrtle – Rectifies the humours. *Patricians* use it, *you* can use it, too! Peloponnesian Syrup of Myrtle – Ask for it by name.

STRABO. "Mee mee mma maaa, mo mo mooo moo...

PELARGON. (*reading from a list*) Topics to be covered at tonight's festivities.

STRABO. *Test* me, I am prepared...

PELARGON. "*Cronax*: his opposition, in the Senate, to the African Campaign."

STRABO. The Tenth African Legion, we see, has just suffered its first defeat, as predicted, *predicted*, mind you, *in* the Senate, by our host, Marcus Rufus Cronax. arch *foe* of The Tenth African Legion...

PELARGON. ...which brings us...

STRABO. I've got it. *I've* got it...

PHILIUS. What do I get to say, Strabo...

STRABO. I've got it, which, naturally, takes me to...which is the house, now...?

(*All look around.*)

PELARGON. It's around here somewhere...

STRABO. Which brings us to...his "tastes"...our host, and his "curious tastes."

PELARGON. You're cutting pretty close to the bone.

STRABO. Cronax is *famed*, alright? For enjoying a bawdy joke at his own expense. He's got a heart as big as the Coliseum...Alright? "Our host, who, as we know, has developed a 'certain proclivity'...I'm not going to say that he 'likes *women*', but, it's been noted that he goes to bed with people who are 'lacking in adjustable equipment... '"

STRABO. uh..."Tenth African *Legion*"...favorite of Caesar... likes "women"...

PELARGON. I'm not sure you can say that and get away with it.

STRABO. "Grasp fortune by the forelock, Pelargon, for she has no hair behind."

(*A door opens before them and a* **MAN** *peers out.*)

STRABO. *Ah.* Here we are...

(*The* **ACTORS** *enter a darkened room lit by torchlight.*)

STRABO. *(entering)* By the gods.

MAN. By the gods!

STRABO. We have arrived.

MAN. We feared the storm would hinder you.

STRABO. I hope my troupe, Sir, knows its duty.

MAN. Bless you.

STRABO. We live to serve.

MAN. Shall I present you...?

STRABO. No, no, why win them over *twice?* You leave the evening in my hands.

(*He leads them to a small dais, before which sits* **TEN MEN**.)

(**STRABO** *takes the stage.*)

PHILIUS. Strabo...

STRABO. Not now. *Gentlemen.* Sorry if we're late. I'm not going to tell you that it's *wet*, but I got a *squid* down my shirt.

(pause, continuing)

And I'd complain, except he was giving me a *hickey*…

(pause)

He was giving me a *hickey*. I, uh…I know, I've got to be careful, touching on *personal* matters. I know our *host*, for example, has, and god knows he's entitled to them, curious tastes"… I'm not saying he likes "women," but…

But we know some of the people he goes to bed with are noticably lacking in adjustable equipment. Or, as the soldiers say, "perhaps they forgot to pack their tent pole."

(deathly silence)

…pack their tent pole…

We're told he made the switch to *women* and on his *wedding* night uttered that timeless phrase: 'I know it's around here *somewhere*…He's had three wives – but that may be because he thought the clitoris was a building in *Greece*.

(pause)

PELARGON. *(prompting)* Tenth African Legion…

PHILIUS. Strabo…

STRABO. Speaking of which, I see where, "too bad," the Tenth African Legion, has suffered its first defeat. You know who *they* are: *they're* the boys their spears come in three sizes, small, medium, and "thank you for a lovely evening."

PHILIUS. Strabo.

STRABO. *(pause)* I see they got their asses whomped and they've been brought home in *shame*, well, what general planned that campaign? He must be one arch shy of an aqueduct…

(pause)

One arch shy of an aqueduct…

(Audience grumbles.)

STRABO. Well, *they'll* have less heads, but *we'll* have more helmets...

PHILIUS. Strabo, we're in the wrong house.

(Audience grumbles.)

PHILIUS *(cont'd)* Cronax lives across the street.

AUDIENCE MEMBER. Kill them all!

PHILIUS. This is the Armory of the Tenth African Legion...

AUDIENCE. *Kill* them, *kill* them, *kill* them... !

(SCENE: INT. DUNGEON ROOM OF THE TENTH AFRICAN LEGION. NIGHT)

(HERALD *enters.)*

HERALD. O Wicked wicked world

How you have wronged me

For my love lies 'crost the

Straits of Messina

O, Fortunate, you pelicans and other wingèd birds

Original verses — no two alike —

Or will write-to-suit –

You only pay for what you use —

Original verses –

We come to you —

(PHILIUS, PELARGON, *and* **STRABO,** *chained to a bench.)*

STRABO. *(pause)* Well, there's some *mistake.*

*(***TITUS,** *a centurion, walks by.)*

STRABO. *Fellow.*

TITUS. What?

STRABO. Fellow, there's some mistake.

TITUS. Well, no. I know that.

STRABO. And I'd like to *ask* you, to bring down, someone in *charge.* So that we may correct this unfortunate misunderstanding. Who's in charge here?

TITUS. Lupus Albus

STRABO. Lupus Albus? The White Wolf of Sardinia…?

TITUS. No. He's long dead. This is his son. Lupus Albus *Secundus,* the White Wolf of Phrygia…

STRABO. Okay, whoever he's the white wolf of, I'd like to ask *him* to come down, so I can explain what I'm sure he will *join* me in laughing at, as a regrettable, but, *amusing* error. You see: we were engaged to perform tonight at the home of Marcus Rufus Cronax, richest man in *Rome.*

TITUS. Yes, his house is across the street...

STRABO. *As* you so wisely note. And, in the *rain*, we, mistakenly, found ourselves *here*...

TITUS. We were expecting *another* group, but they were delayed by the rain.

STRABO. Delayed by the rain, were they.

TITUS. But they've arrived now...

STRABO. Another troupe of *actors?*

TITUS. No. Of priests.

STRABO. ...priests.

TITUS. ...who are now conducting the funeral service.

(*pause*)

STRABO. The funeral service.

TITUS. Yes. The most solemn last rites for lost Brothers in Arms of the Tenth African Legion.

(*pause*)

Which sacred rites you have profaned.

(**TITUS** *exits.*)

STRABO. ...*alright*...*Pelargon*...

PELARGON. Don't talk to me...

PHILIUS. Strabo: *are* we going to Sicily?

STRABO. *Alright.* Here's my plan. *Here* is my plan: We are, are we not? The valued, the *beloved* friends of who? Pelargon? Of who?

PHILIUS. Of who, Strabo...

STRABO. Of Marcus Rufus Cronax, richest man in Rome, who, at this very minute...

(*They stop. At the entrance is* **LUPUS ALBUS,** *the White Wolf of Phrygia, backed by* **TITUS** *and* **TWO CENTURIONS.**)

STRABO. Sir, Sir? *We* are the beloved friends of your *neighbor.* Marcus Rufus Cronax. Richest...

LUPUS ALBUS. Centurion...

TITUS. Quiet before Lupus Albus.

(**TITUS** exits.)

(pause)

LUPUS ALBUS. Were you sent by Cronax? Cronax do you say?

STRABO. Yes, Sir. Yes, Sir. We are in the pay of Cronax.

LUPUS ALBUS. Sent by him?

STRABO. Yes!

LUPUS ALBUS. Cronax, our staunchest foe. In the Senate...?

STRABO. He's in the "Senate," do you say?

LUPUS ALBUS. As all the world knows –

STRABO. All the world but us poor actors – Ha ha ha, no, god forbid we get involved in Politics...

LUPUS ALBUS. Indeed?

STRABO. Oh, please. We are as innocent of politics as the Babe Unborn.

LUPUS ALBUS. Then, you say, you do not know of our disgrace...

PHILIUS. I tried to tell you.

STRABO. Your disgrace? No. No. I know nothing but your interminable Career of Martial Glory! Oh, Mighty Scourge of...

PELARGON. Phrygia...

STRABO. Oh, mighty Scourge of Phrygia.

LUPUS ALBUS. And, you alone, in all Rome, are ignorant of our First Defeat?

STRABO. First defeat? No.

PHILIUS. No, Strabo, you heard about that...

STRABO. The Tenth African Legion fail?

PHILIUS. Strabo, you know that...

STRABO. The young child is insane, and "we keep him by us, as a reminder of the fragility of all things."

LUPUS ALBUS. You did not know, we had been recalled to Rome to suffer disgrace and decimation before Caesar

STRABO. May the gods decree otherwise...oh, Sir...

LUPUS ALBUS. ...which disgrace was ordained by that swine, *Cronax*...

STRABO. ...a curse upon his seed...

LUPUS ALBUS. Who stood in the Senate and demanded that decimation...to which we go at sunrise?

STRABO. May the sun, Sir, which rises upon the disgrace of the Tenth African Legion live to rue the day.

(*pause*)

LUPUS ALBUS. Have you not uttered sufficient blasphemy.

STRABO. *Blasphemy...*

LUPUS ALBUS. You have spewed your bawdy filth at the sacred observance of the Funeral Ode for Fallen Comrades.

STRABO. I plead to spend. The remainder of my life in expiation.

(**TITUS** *enters. Men grumble offstage.*)

TITUS. Sir, the men, in their rage, are clamoring for the actors' blood.

LUPUS ALBUS. Clamoring for blood are they...? Let's give them blood, then – to cleanse this vile blasphemy.

STRABO. Uh...

LUPUS ALBUS. (*to* **TITUS**) Kill them all...

(**LUPUS ALBUS** *turns to go.*)

STRABO. Wait, Sir! Wait.

(**LUPUS ALBUS** *turns back.*)

LUPUS ALBUS. My thoughts are elsewhere.

STRABO. Just the One Moment, if I may.

(*pause*)

I am an *actor*, Sir, whose life, at *best*, is a series of shams. We neither farm, nor hunt. We are debarred from bearing arms. By those who *toil* in the world we are despised. Except for that one moment, when we are permitted, on the stage, to make them laugh. Or cry.

In sympathy. Not even with ourselves. Good, Sir, but for that better being we impersonate. For we, ourselves, are nothing.

(pause)

And we have offended you: who bleed for the state. And should we, having wronged you, suffer at your hands: though, in our weakness, we may weep, in our deeper soul we know the punishment is just...turn, Turn, ye gods. Your face now toward us. Now away – howe'er your visage shines, your hand is on us all.

(pause)

LUPUS ALBUS. Your name, Actor.

STRABO. Sir, I am but Strabo.

LUPUS ALBUS. That speech...

STRABO. Sir...

LUPUS ALBUS. Is it not from "The Methathon" by *Plautus?*

STRABO. Your honor's learning is outpaced only by his bravery.

LUPUS ALBUS. Yes. Thank you. How would you describe that speech?

STRABO. It is a humble plea for mercy.

(pause)

LUPUS ALBUS. You asked how you might make right your offense.

STRABO. Bid me, Sir...and the tide shall obey the moon.

LUPUS ALBUS. My Tenth African Legion is to appear, tomorrow, before Caesar. In disgrace...

STRABO. May all the gods, in their combined omnipotence...

LUPUS ALBUS. ...indeed...Might you. On our *behalf...give* that speech. In our name. To Caesar...?

(pause)

To plead for us.

STRABO. Give the speech...before Caesar...?

LUPUS ALBUS. *Yes.*

STRABO. *Plead* before *Caesar?*

LUPUS ALBUS. Yes.

STRABO. Sir, were I to live ten thousand lives, I could not wish, *in* them, for any greater honor...

TITUS. But General.

LUPUS ALBUS. Yes, Titus.

(**TITUS** *takes* **LUPUS ALBUS** *aside and whispers.*)

LUPUS ALBUS. *(to the* **TITUS***)* What? (**TITUS** *whispers again*)

(*pause*)

Yes, thank you.

(**LUPUS ALBUS,** *sadly, turns back to the troupe.*)

LUPUS ALBUS. I am reminded that as per the pandect of Justina, the audience with Caesar is closed.

STRABO. Closed. Oh no.

PELARGON. Closed, what does that mean...?

LUPUS ALBUS. Only the members of the summoned Legion may attend the Imperial audience.

TITUS. General.

(**TITUS** *whispers to* **LUPUS.***)*

STRABO. What is he saying... .

LUPUS ALBUS. *(to* **TITUS***)* ...in what capacity?

(**TITUS** *whispers some more.*)

LUPUS ALBUS. *(to* **STRABO***)* He has reminded me. Of the position of Auxiliary...

PELARGON. Auxiliary, what is that...?

LUPUS ALBUS. *(to* **TITUS***)* But, that hasn't been employed in *years*... I doubt...

STRABO. ...we'll do it.

(**TITUS** *whispers to* **LUPUS ALBUS.***)*

PELARGON. What is it?

LUPUS ALBUS. I am reminded that, as per our *charter*, should one, of his Own Free Will, pledge himself...

STRABO. ...we'll do it.

LUPUS ALBUS. ...pledge himself to the Tenth African Legion.

STRABO. We'll do it.

LUPUS ALBUS. He may be *inducted*, as Auxiliary Member.

STRABO. Count me in, count *us* in.

PELARGON. Don't do it.

STRABO. What do we have to do...?

PELARGON. Don't do it...

LUPUS ALBUS. Say the pledge, bare the breast, and suffer the Solemn Ceremonial Blow.

STRABO. ...the Solemn Ceremonial Blow?

PELARGON. I told you.

STRABO. No, uh, Pelargon, explain to him why. "The Solemn Ceremonial Blow..." would not actually be the "thing," you know, and the kid's getting over a cold. So, to bare his breast...

LUPUS ALBUS. ...which Blow may, by statute, "neither cause pain, nor draw blood."

STRABO. The "Solemn Ceremonial Blow," as I was saying, is that blow I seek. Induct us then, O, Scourge of Phrygia, and let us plead your case before mighty Caesar!

LUPUS ALBUS. *(receiving the ceremonial sword)* Kneel then and bare your breast.

PELARGON. I don't like it.

STRABO. It can't cause pain nor draw blood – alright?

(They kneel and bare their breasts.)

LUPUS ALBUS. "By the hilt of that sword which won Rome from the wilderness. The Legion forever." Say it.

ALL. "By the hilt of that sword which won Rome from the wilderness. The Legion forever."

(He touches the side of the sword to their chests lightly.)

LUPUS ALBUS. Arise, Auxiliary Members of the Tenth African Legion.

(They rise.)

STRABO. Oh, how the world shines new-formed, to a member of this noble band...

LUPUS ALBUS. Enjoy your rest, my brothers. For tomorrow, you stand before Caesar. Unshackle them.

STRABO. *(to* **PELARGON***)* Well, what did I tell you, you're always looking on the dark side...

(to **LUPUS ALBUS***)*

Oh, Great Praetor. Lupus Albus...White Wolf of Phrygia...

(He turns back, and **LUPUS** *and his men are gone.)*

STRABO. Gaius Paulus, you're *better* off drowned, cause who's gonna be the favorite of Caesar? And the cork merchants in Sicily can hire Gaius Paulus, dead though he is...

PELARGON. Don't defame the dead.

STRABO. Because tomorrow morning, *we*, Auxiliary members of the Tenth African Legion...

*(***TITUS** *enters with two other men in military attire.)*

PELARGON. ...who is this...?

TITUS. This here's the armorer.

(The **ARMORER'S ASSISTANT** *begins taking measurements. First* **PHILIUS***, then* **PELARGON***, then* **STRABO***.)*

STRABO. Ah. Yes, my comrade, yes. The armorer, who, no doubt has come to strike off our shackles.

TITUS. ...who's come to measure you for your ceremonial attire...

PELARGON. Ceremonial attire?

STRABO. Our *armor*, Pelargon...*armor* – as befits members of the Legion!

PHILIUS. ...we get a suit of *armor*...?

ARMORER. Chest?

ARMORER'S ASSISTANT. *(as he measures each of the men)* Thirty-eight. Forty-one. Forty-six.

ARMORER. Waist?

ARMORER'S ASSISTANT. *(measuring)* Twenty-nine. Thirty-eight. Forty-two.

ARMORER. *(to STRABO)* Watch that mead!!

STRABO. *(pats his belly)* Well, you know...

PHILIUS. We get a suit of armor. Oh good!

TITUS. *(to the armorer)* You forgot to do the neckpiece.

ARMORER. *(departing)* No, they won't need the neckpiece.

TITUS. Oh, that's right.

PHILIUS. Why won't we need the neckpiece?

ARMORER. *(exiting)* 'Cause if you're wearing the neckpiece, your head won't fit on the chopping block.

    (exits)

STRABO. I think I'm missing something.

PELARGON. Why would they put our head on the chopping block?

TITUS. To chop off your head.

STRABO. Yes, thank you. Uh...

    (to TITUS)

    Could you explain this to us?

TITUS. ...*you* know.

PELARGON. Pretend we don't know, and tell us.

TITUS. Caesar...?

PHILIUS. ...yes...?

TITUS. ...as you know, recalled the Tenth African Legion to *Rome*...

PHILIUS. ...we know that.

TITUS. Because we suffered an inglorious defeat.

STRABO. Yes that's regrettable.

TITUS. And in such cases...

PELARGON. ...oh no.

TITUS. The offending Legion. Must choose amongst itself.

PHILIUS. ...um mmm...

PELARGON. ...oh, no...

TITUS. Three members.

PHILIUS. Oh, that would be us!

TITUS. To be publicly beheaded.

(pause; exits)

PHILIUS. But, if you chop off our heads, we'll *die...*

PELARGON. Will somebody shut that kid up.

Scene Three

(**SCENE:** *MORNING IN THE CELL.*)

(*The* **HERALD** *passes outside the window.*)

HERALD. See how the headsman's scaffold on the grass Salutes the wakeful as night steals away Each knows though all forget that life must pass How fortunate the man who knows the day. Bactrian "Lynx Brand" opium. Lynx Brand opium. Look for the shining eyes on every packet. Get high and stay high, with Bactrian Lynx Brand opium.

(**STRABO** *pacing back and forth. The other two sitting on their cells. A rooster crows.*)

STRABO. Alright: Here's my plan.

(*to* **PELARGON**)

"Wake up, wake up, wake up:" "The kid has a tummy-ache." The Guard? "Help help help, this lovely young lad is in agony…" so on…the Guard comes in, we hit him on the head…

PELARGON. And then what?

STRABO. We dress up as the guard.

PELARGON. "*We* dress up as the guard?"

STRABO. Well, yes. *One* of us…

PELARGON. …It's futile, Strabo. We're inside a *dungeon.* Surrounded. By the best-armed, most ferocious, and angriest men in Rome. Who are they angry at? They're angry at *us.*

STRABO. Let's…

PELARGON. And, Strabo, I am angry at *you.* I'm *tired.* They're going to cut my head off in a half-hour, and I don't feel well.

PHILIUS. I'm frightened, Strabo.

STRABO. Hush, my Secluded Vale of Acanthis. Would I let anything befall you?

PHILIUS. They're going to kill us, Strabo.

STRABO. Not while the Ichor of Imagination pulses through my veins.

PHILIUS. …and I wish I'd been better to you. What did you ask? I could have made you happy.

STRABO. Thank you.

PHILIUS. It's just that you're so *old.*

STRABO. Uh huh.

PHILIUS. If you'd been *younger…*

STRABO. Hm.

PHILIUS. Or better looking…

STRABO. Yes…I've got to think…

(**TITUS** *enters.*)

STRABO. No, no, the hour is not yet at hand. *No…*

TITUS. Na, I've got some news. I've got some good news and some *bad* news.

PELARGON. …tell us the news.

TITUS. Caesar has reconsidered. Your sentence has been *changed*!

STRABO. Our sentence has been changed. Oh, Zeus, Oh, merciful Mars, god of War, who, in his wisdom…our sentence has been changed!

PELARGON. What's the *bad* news?

TITUS. That *is* the bad news.

PHILIUS. They were going to cut our heads off. What could be worse news than that?

TITUS. Caesar has decided you are not to have your heads cut off as that is too merciful a death.

PELARGON. What's he gonna do instead?

TITUS. You are to be castrated, and drawn and quartered.

(*pause*)

They hang you for about a half an hour, then, they cut you down, and cut out your entrails and put out your eyes, *then…*

STRABO. Yes, that's quite alright.

TITUS. No, then it gets interesting, they...

PELARGON. *(interrupting)* Why did they change the sentence?

TITUS. *Caesar...*

STRABO. ...yes?

TITUS. Already incensed at the defeat of the Tenth African...

PELARGON. Yes, yes, we know that...

TITUS. Is further maddened by the loss, at sea, of the Troupe of Gaius Paulus. His favorite actors.

> *(pause)*

STRABO. *Oh.*

PELARGON. What's the good news?

TITUS. The *good* news...

> *(confidentially)*

> ...is that I've *managed*...at some personal expense...

> *(produces goblet from under his cloak)*

> ...to sneak you in *this*...

PELARGON. What is it?

PHILIUS. ...it's a cup.

TITUS. It is a "cup of wine." But, what is *in* the cup?

PHILIUS. *(pause)* "Wine."

TITUS. Yes, but what's in the wine?

STRABO. What's in the wine?

TITUS. ...Opium. There's enough opium in here, to kill a horse. If *each* of you, drinks just one *mouthful*, you'll be fine, when, when...

> *(offers the cup to* **STRABO***)*

PELARGON. I'd like my sip *now*, please.

STRABO. Wait, but, to quaff that cup would be tantamount to surrender...

TITUS. You bet.

STRABO. ...not while I have a plan.

PELARGON. I'd like my sip now, please.

STRABO. That's why, you see, *that's* why you never amounted to anything, Pelargon...

PHILIUS. *(to* **PELARGON***)* You told me you never amounted to anything because Strabo held you back out of jealousy...

STRABO. Oh, how *cheap*, Pelargon. How tawdry. Who has shared good and bad with you for twenty years. *Now* it comes out. Now. Facing death. Yes, *take* your sip. *Quitter*...Yes. Face death as you faced life – *cravenly. Abjectly.* Take your sip.

PELARGON. Thank you. I will – gimme the cup.

*(***RAMUS*** enters.)*

RAMUS. By the gods.

STRABO. Yeah, by the gods. And what is the thought. I will bear. To my death?

RAMUS. Good morning.

STRABO. Your ingratitude. No. I do not *need* the opium, to dull my senses. *You* have dulled my senses.

*(***TITUS*** starts to exit)*

No, no. I'll *take* the opium...thank you.

TITUS. Two sesterces...

STRABO. *What?*

TITUS. I can't give it to you for *nothing*. 'F I get caught, it's my *job*...

PHILIUS. Good morning, Ramus...

RAMUS. Good morning...

STRABO. I don't *have* two sesterces.

TITUS. *(takes back the cup)* Sorry.

STRABO. Wait, wait, wait. Isn't there anything...

(pause)

TITUS. Lend me the kid for one half-hour.

STRABO. You want me to trade this child for the cup of opium?

TITUS. Yes…

PELARGON. *Done.* Philius…?

TITUS. Thank you.

STRABO. No, wait…

PELARGON. Philius, this fellow wants to tell you some of his war stories…

STRABO. Yes, no, wait, that wouldn't be a good idea.

TITUS. Sounds like a good idea to me.

STRABO. Noo, you can't have the child.

TITUS. Why not?

STRABO. Uh…his virginity is pledged to the Goddess Demeter.

TITUS. His Virginity is Pledged to the Goddess Demeter…?

STRABO. As I have said…but *this* man (of Pelargon) Skilled in the Arts of Love…

RAMUS. I can attest to that…

STRABO. …this man…

TITUS. Ramus…?

RAMUS. Titus…? You know when I got up this morning…

STRABO. Will you shut up. Why did they let you in…?

TITUS. Let him in? Do you know who this *is*?

PELARGON. No.

TITUS. This is Ramus, who fought with the Tenth African Legion in the Snows.

PHILIUS. What were you doing in the Snows?

TITUS. We were lost.

STRABO. You were in the Tenth African Legion…?

TITUS. *In* the Legion…? He saved the life of Lupus Albus Primus, the *original* White Wolf of Sardinia, whose *son*, the White Wolf of Phrygia, is our General today.

STRABO. He saved the life of the General's father…

TITUS. Who, on his deathbed, yes, clasped to his bosom, his young son and said, "What e'er this soldier, Ramus, desires in life, my son, *grant* it to him."

STRABO. Hold on now, and slow it down, the White Wolf of Phrygia, is pledged to grant this old bum's wish...?

TITUS. ...for anything under heaven.

PELARGON. Do you think I could have that opium?

STRABO. BY ALL THE GODS AT ONCE – Good Ramus. Intercede for us, with Lupus Albus, that stern, though worthy commander who holds our lives in his hand.

RAMUS. Alright.

STRABO. Oh, thank you. Thank you.

RAMUS. But the one thing I came to tell you:

STRABO. *Yes?*

RAMUS. The coin you gave me...

STRABO. The coin I gave you?

RAMUS. —yeah, when you bought that *charm?*

STRABO. ...Alright...

RAMUS. ...it's counterfeit.

STRABO. I'll make it right.

RAMUS. And I was concerned, that if you paid for a good luck charm with a bad *coin*, you might have Bad Luck.

STRABO. What truth there is in your words.

(*to* **TITUS**)

Call your Commander. To hear this Good Man's Appeal. Oh, Ye gods, who lovingly grant absolution to the Deepest Sinner. Thank you from one who has, yet again, unearned, received your Grace.

RAMUS. I'll drink to that.

(**RAMUS** *grabs the goblet, drinks and falls down in a stupor. All stand around looking at the fallen* **RAMUS.**)

PHILIUS. Oh, dear...

TITUS. *(pause)* Did he drink it all?

PELARGON. Yes.

TITUS. There's enough opium in there to sedate an aurochs.

STRABO. ...An aurochs...??

TITUS. As I have said.

STRABO. Could we get some more, please?

(DRUM BEATS.)

TITUS. Nope. We're out of time. There's the death drum.

(The drum beats again.)

TITUS. And so it's time for your execution.

*(As **TITUS** leaves the dungeon.)*

TITUS. FALL BACK, AND CLEAR THE PATH OF THE CONDEMNED.

(The drumbeat continues.)

TITUS. CAESAR, IN HIS MERCY, GRANTS THEM ONE LAST MOMENT FOR REFLECTION.

PELARGON. ...well.

*(**STRABO** comes downstage to orate.)*

STRABO. "Yes, I have sinned. For I am mortal. And the gods know that all mortals sin and so inform us, taxing the sinner with that which he mis-names 'ill fortune.' But for its better name is Justice. How find we ourselves upon this stranded shore? The failure of a rope, whose loss split the sail? An inclement conjunction of wind and the tide? A moment's folly inspiring the youth to seek his fortune on the sea... Until co-merged with that salt element, he knew himself unfitted for the regularity of Earth. Which bore him. And, in a half a glass may mourn him..."

(pause)

PELARGON. *(prompting)* "See the Phoenicians mass..."

STRABO. "See the Phoenicians mass upon the mottled shore..."

OFFSTAGE VOICE (GUARD). Members of the Tenth Legion, prepare to meet your doom!

PHILIUS. Strabo...

STRABO. Yes, goodbye, child.

PHILIUS. Goodbye.

STRABO. Perhaps we shall meet again. Beyond the river

PHILIUS. I hope so, but.

STRABO. Yes. In that happy land...

PHILIUS. Yes, but...

STRABO. Where there are no more critics

PHILIUS. Yes, there's just the one thing...

STRABO. What, child, what?

PHILIUS. You shouldn't have given the old man a fake coin.

TITUS. *(O.S.)* Helmets off, greet those who, for their comrades sake, must suffer death!

PHILIUS. Because, if you'd given him a real coin, perhaps our luck would not have changed.

(**TITUS**, *the burly guards and the priest arrive, helmets off, and open the gates.*)

PRIEST. O Mighty Mars, prepare to receive unto your care, the mutilated bodies of these, your servants...

PHILIUS. Strabo...

GUARD. Are the condemned men prepared...?

PHILIUS. Give him a coin, Strabo. Give the old man a coin.

STRABO. What?

PHILIUS. You cheated him of his coin for the good luck charm. Don't let that be on your soul, before... before...

(**PHILIUS** *weeps.*)

STRABO. No, child I would not die with that upon my soul.

(*to* **TITUS**)

Give me a coin.

TITUS. Bind them, and Hood them, and Draw them Forth.

STRABO. Give me a coin, for the Love of God.

TITUS. Why should I give you a coin?

STRABO. Lend me a coin.

TITUS. You'll be dead in half an hour.

STRABO. Then you can take it *back*...

TITUS. No, that's true...

>   *(hands him a coin)*

>   Just for the half hour, mind...

>   *(TITUS exits. STRABO hands the coin to RAMUS.)*

STRABO. Ramus, Ramus, wake up.

RAMUS. ...what...?

STRABO. Here's the coin I owe you.

>   *(pause)*

>   For the Good Luck *Charm?* Ramus? For the Good *Luck* charm...?

>   *(beat)*

RAMUS. *(waking)* ...the coin for the good-luck charm.

>   *(We hear a drum roll offstage.)*

GUARD. It's time.

>   *(The guards begin to bind the three. TITUS exits.)*

PHILIUS. I'm sorry that I wouldn't go to bed with you, Strabo.

STRABO. That's alright.

PELARGON. I'm sorry that I *did*...

PHILIUS. And I regret I never knew the joy. Of acting with you. On stage.

PELARGON. Let the boy dream.

GUARD. Make way for the condemned!

>   *(They engage in a group hug. The drum gives a final roll.)*

STRABO. *(To PHILIUS)* Goodbye, young lad, farewell, beauty.

PHILIUS. Goodbye, Strabo.

STRABO. *(To PELARGON)* Goodbye, Old Comrade.

PELARGON. I'm two years younger than you.

STRABO. But I've aged better.

PELARGON. Die with dignity.

STRABO. *(Sighs; Pause)* Come, friends, let's show them how to make an exit...

(They start toward the door.)

TITUS. *(entering)* Great news, great news, great news!

(beat)

The Troupe of the actor Gaius Paulus, favorite of Caesar, believed lost at sea, has been found alive!

STRABO. The day lacked only *that* to be complete.

TITUS. In honor of which, Caesar has remitted punishment for all crimes. Up to, and including that, decreed for the Tenth Legion!!!

(pause; to the three actors)

You are all free to go!!!

*(A beat. All exit the cell, save the three actors and the drugged **RAMUS**. The three start toward the door. Beat. **STRABO** turns back.)*

STRABO. *(to **PELARGON**; re: **RAMUS**)* ...get the coin back.

Scene Four

(SCENE: *MORNING – THE STUDIO OF STRABO.*)

(*The* HERALD *walks by outside the studio, in which we find* STRABO *and* PHILIUS.)

HERALD. Oh Rome arise and welcome that new day The gods have decreed for our disport Work, frolic, suffer, sin and pray In the bright courtyard of the sombre court Arise ye nobles, citizens, and slaves Some to dig gardens, others to dig graves, For whilst the sun...

STRABO. *(shouting out)* Oh, not *today*, not *today*, *would* you please? Work is at hand, *love* is in the air, and nobody in a good mood ever listened to philosophy.

(*A HORN is heard, offstage.*)

HERALD. *(going off)* Hark to the second herald of the Morn The Packet boat's departure horn

Make haste, Make haste down to the Quay

If you are bound for Sicelay...

STRABO. Oh, stuff a sock in it.

HERALD. Tunics and togas. Bernstein Brand tunics and togas. Made by philosophers. "They Just wear on and on." Buy Bernstein Brand tunics and togas.

(*The* HERALD *moves off.*)

STRABO. *(to* PHILIUS*)* Continue.

PHILIUS. *(declaiming)* "What is more precious than wine, you ask? What is more precious than wine...?"

(PELARGON *enters with letters.*)

PELARGON. *(to* STRABO*)* I've got the suitcases strapped up.

(gesturing off)

STRABO. One moment.

(to PHILIUS*)*

Say it simply, like it's just *occurred* to you.

PHILIUS. *(nods)* "What is more precious than wine...? You *ask* me: I will tell you Cork."

STRABO. *(pause)* Cork.

PHILIUS. I'm here to *learn.* You bid me, *whatever* you bid me, Strabo, *that* I shall do.

PELARGON. His father's late with the tuition.

STRABO. No matter. We'll be paid in *Sicily*...Keep it up, lad, keep it up.

PHILIUS. "What is more precious than wine? Mff mff. Cork." "For without Cork, what *good* is wine...? Answer me that, good citizens of Sicily."

STRABO. That is it, my lad. *Look* them in the eye, and *make* them answer you that.

PHILIUS. God bless you, Strabo...

STRABO. And you, my Little Lamb.

PHILIUS. You are a wise mentor.

STRABO. Where, in this spotted life have I heard words as sweet...?

PHILIUS. I look forward to our time in Sicily

STRABO. As do I, my amphora of honeyed mead.

PHILIUS. Will you teach me to swim?

STRABO. I shall teach you all sorts of gymnastics.

(There is a knock at the door.)

STRABO. Ah – That would be the stevedores come for our baggage...

PHILIUS. I'll get it. "Haste then, young champion, to the Gate of Acharnia, and report what messenger, and with what intent, disturbs our disport..."

(PHILIUS exits).

STRABO. *(to PELARGON)* Well he's willing, he's *young*, he's beautiful, and perhaps he'll learn.

PELARGON. And perhaps the sun, in search of novelty, will rise in the west.

STRABO. How ill your cynicism becomes you.

PELARGON. Really...

STRABO. I need a drink before the ship.

(They go off. There is a knock at the door.

PHILIUS *goes to the door.)*

PHILIUS. *(he opens the door)* Welcome to the Studio of Strabo... What errand brings you to our door...?

LANDLORD. I've come for the rent.

PHILIUS. Aha.

(The **LANDLORD** *enters with a LETTER which he hands to* **PHILIUS.***)*

LANDLORD. And the postman handed me this letter for your master.

PHILIUS. He and Pelargon have stepped out for a drink.

LANDLORD. How may they drink, being perpetually impoverished?

PHILIUS. They drink upon credit, Sir. As we have been given an engagement.

LANDLORD. An *engagement*?

PHILIUS. Sir, as I have said.

LANDLORD. Where?

PHILIUS. In a half-hour we sail. To open the Sicilian Cork Festival.

LANDLORD. ...you sail for Sicily...

PHILIUS. ...that's where they're holding it.

(RAMUS enters.)

RAMUS. By the gods...

LANDLORD. *(to PHILIUS)* You're *leaving...*?

RAMUS. Might anyone gain merit by giving an old soldier some wine...

(STRABO and PELARGON enter with a flagon.)

PELARGON. I'll share my wine with you, Good Soul. And then Farewell.

RAMUS. Where are you off to?

STRABO. Sicily.

LANDLORD. You're going to Sicily?

STRABO. Fear not for your rent, O font of avarice, it shall be *sent* to you…Yes, the Sicilians impressed by our status as Auxiliary Members of the Tenth African Legion have engaged us to open the Sicilian Cork Festival.

RAMUS. Everyone's going to Sicily…

(He drinks the wine.)

STRABO. What do you mean?

RAMUS. Down at the docks. The Troupe of Gaius Paulus. Has just been engaged. To open the Sicilian Cork Festival…

(RAMUS takes a nap)

STRABO. What…?

PHILIUS. *(producing the letter)* Oh, Strabo. The Landlord brought you a letter.

PELARGON. *(takes the letter and reads)* "Please accept our regrets. The untimely resurrection to life of the Troupe of Gaius Paulus has forced us to rescind your offer of employment. Thank you for your interest in our festival."

(pause)

STRABO. …they gave our spot to *Paulus*…

(pause)

LANDLORD. I…

STRABO. No, please. Please, *evict* us, Landlord. To die hungry in the streets cursed by the Gods, whom, it seems, we have irremediably offended.

(pause)

LANDLORD. Then you won't be going to Sicily.

STRABO. *(as to a child)* It seems the Sicilians, mistaking Renown for Merit, have given our spot to Gaius Paulus…

PHILIUS. …that hack.

STRABO. Chide me, O Fortune. I remain your fool. Let years of effort in your service count for naught. Exalt mine enemies and grind, beneath your heel, your slave.

LANDLORD. I grieve to hear of your reversal.

STRABO. The loss is not mine alone, nay, but that of the denizens of Sicily, forever denied our performance

PELARGON. The Gods Grant them Forbearance.

STRABO. Had I but Funds, O ye Gods. I would transport *my* troupe to Sicily, and challenge Paulus. By the Gods, I would *enter* the Pageant unpaid and unmask him before all the world,as a usurper.

LANDLORD. What a spectacle that would bid fair to be.

STRABO. As you so rightly note. Did the world but turn in service of justice...

LANDLORD. Had you but funds.

STRABO. Yes. But no. They praise the Candle who need but ope the shutters to behold the sun...

PHILIUS. Be strong, Strabo... *(pause)*

LANDLORD. True worth is often overlooked.

STRABO. The wonder is it's ever remarked.

LANDLORD. Take the Lad, for instance.

STRABO. ...the lad...

LANDLORD. Yes. Might I talk with you a moment.

(The **LANDLORD** *draws him outside for a moment, leaving* **PHILIUS** *and* **PELARGON.***)*

PHILIUS. I would have liked to go to Sicily...

PELARGON. Yes.

PHILIUS. Strabo said he was going to teach me to swim.

PELARGON. No doubt.

PHILIUS. Pelargon, Do you think that I have talent?

PELARGON. Son, You have that which is far rarer than talent.

PHILIUS. What is that?

PELARGON. A cheerful outlook.

PHILIUS. Yes, but I'll have to go home now. And go into the Myrrh business

PELARGON. There'll always be a need for Myrrh.

PHILIUS. That's true. But now I'll never learn to act.

PELARGON. Son, it's a life of disappointment. Talent is overlooked, youth vanishes, and we mourn not only the caprices of fate, but our own, willful, squandered opportunities.

(pause)

But I've enjoyed our time together.

PHILIUS. Thank you, Pelargon.

(**STRABO** *and the* **LANDLORD** *reenter.*)

STRABO. Recall the stevedores! Our bags to the boat. For we take ship for Sicily...

PHILIUS. For Sicily?

STRABO. The Troupe of Strabo is to perform at the Sicilian Cork Festival!

PELARGON. Where did the Troupe of Strabo get the money...?

PHILIUS. For Sicily? Oh Strabo, Hurrah! Hurrah!

PELARGON. Where did the Troupe of Strabo get the money...?

PHILIUS. Oh, Strabo, how I admire you!

STRABO. I hope, I sincerely hope, my acolyte, you, whose devotion has warmed, if not my nether parts, that higher portion of this earthly self.

PHILIUS. Your heart?

STRABO. Yes. You have warmed my heart, Young Philius. And, lad, in Sicily...

PHILIUS. How did we get the fare for Sicily...?

STRABO. ...the fare for Sicily...

PHILIUS. Yes.

STRABO. *(brings the landlord forward) This* man, Young Philius. This Patron of the Arts, has, in his unexampled generosity, funded our passage.

PELARGON. ...why?

STRABO. Nor is this all. He undertakes, Young Philius, to continue your tutelage.

PHILIUS. My tutelage?

STRABO. Yes.

PHILIUS. …the Landlord's coming with us to Sicily…?

STRABO. No, you're not going to Sicily. You're staying here.

PHILIUS. We're not going to Sicily?

STRABO. No, Lad. Beautiful lad. *I* must go to Sicily, while you remain.

PHILIUS. Without *you*, Strabo…?

STRABO. *(aside)* Oh, break, my heart…

   (to **PHILIUS** *)*

   Without me, yes, but *this* fine man…

   (of **LANDLORD** *)*

   …is pledged to instruct you in the noblest of Life's Mysteries.

PHILIUS. The Landlord's going to teach me to act?

STRABO. No, you're going into Real Estate.

RAMUS. *(Arising from hir torpor)* In *this* market?

End